HORSES & PONIES ACTIVITY BOOK

INTRODUCTION TO HORSES & HORSEBACK RIDING

Created & Illustrated by Susan DiFelice

Visit www.allpony.com for horse & pony education,
young rider games, quizzes, products, and free printables.

HORSEBACK RIDING SAFETY

Practicing safe riding principles and good barn manners can lead to many years of happy, healthy riding enjoyment. Always ride under the supervision of an adult and wear the following:

Long pants or breeches

ASTM International & Safety Equipment Institute (ASTM/SEI) approved riding helmet

Sturdy shoes or boots, above the ankle in height, with a hard sole and 1" heel

Most horseback riding barns have rules posted in order to keep everyone happy and safe. Riding can be dangerous and most stables will ask visitors to be mindful of the following:

- You may be asked to sign a release form.

- Always clean up after yourself and your horse.

- Return all tack and stable supplies to the correct location.

- No yelling or running while at the barn.

- Always keep gates and stall doors closed and latched.

- Don't use tack or belongings that belong to other people unless you have their permission.

- Respect the barn hours of operation.

Remember to have fun and be safe!

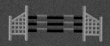

PICTURE SEARCH

Look for these pictures in the activity book.

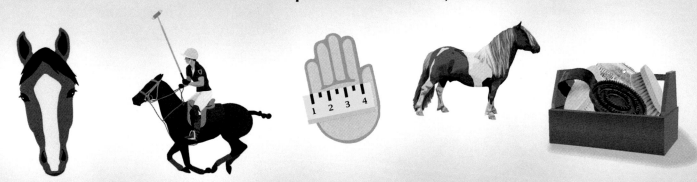

PONY BARN MIX-UP

Four ponies need to find their barns. Which pony belongs to which barn? Start at a pony and follow the path to find out.

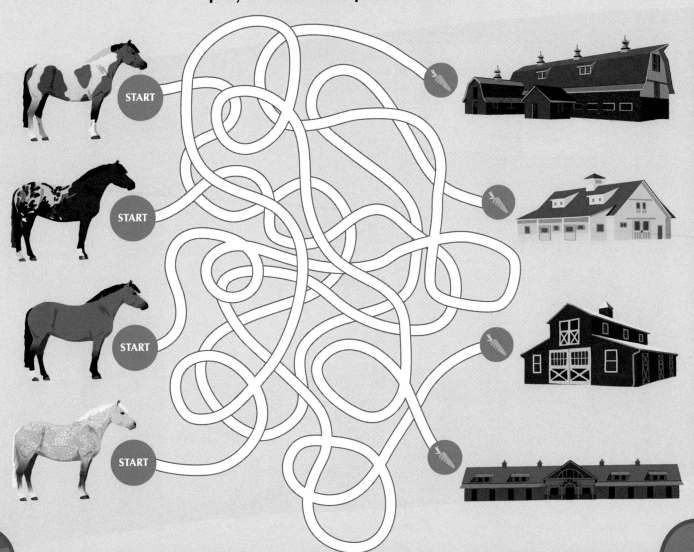

PAPER PONY DOLL

Cut out the ponies, saddle pads, saddles, leg wraps and neck ribbons along the dotted lines. Fold the flaps around the pony to tack it up!

GROOMING

WHY DO WE GROOM HORSES?

- To check for injuries or problems
- To prevent sores caused from dirt under tack
- To promote good circulation of the blood
- It feels good to the horse
- To condition the horse's skin and make the coat shiny

THE ORDER OF GROOMING

1. **CURRY COMB:** Curry comb the coat in a circular motion to break up mud and loosen dirt from the surface of the skin. Start at the top of the neck and work your way down the body. Do not use the curry comb on the head or lower legs.

2. **DANDY BRUSH:** The dandy brush, or hard brush, flicks away dirt that the curry comb loosened. Start at the top of the neck and work your way down the rest of the horse. Avoid using on sensitive areas of skin.

3. **BODY BRUSH:** Also known as a Soft Brush. Cleans away the dust and dirt that was loosened by the dandy brush and curry comb, and is used to keep the horse's coat clean & shiny. Brush in the direction of the hair and clean the brush after every few strokes.

4. **MANE & TAIL:** Pick out twigs and hay, and separate the tangles by hand, one section at a time. Use a hair brush, plastic comb or dandy brush to remove the tangles. Start at the bottom and work your way up. Try to avoid breaking or pulling the hair. When brushing the tail, always stand to one side of the horse. Brush the mane to the right side of the neck.

5. **PICK HOOVES:** Pick out the hooves and check each shoe to make sure they are on tight. Brush dirt and mud off the exterior of the hooves.

GROOMING TOOLS MATCH GAME

Draw a line from the name to the correct grooming tool.

MANE COMB

DANDY BRUSH

CURRY COMB

HOOF PICK

BODY BRUSH

ENGLISH OR WESTERN?

Tack is the equipment or accessories used when working with and riding horses and ponies. Tack includes saddles, stirrups, bridles, halters, reins, and bits. Putting a saddle and bridle on a horse is referred to as "tacking up". The room that stores tack inside a stable is called a tack room. The two basic types of saddles are: **English** and **Western**.

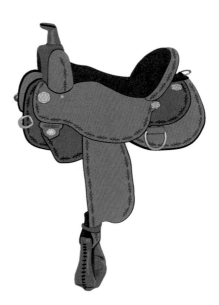

ENGLISH SADDLES

English saddles are all purpose saddles: a cross between jumping and dressage saddles. They are an excellent choice for first time riders as they allow you to try out different riding sports.

WESTERN SADDLES

Western saddles are used in western riding sports such as barrel racing and rodeos. Also, it is the preferred saddle for dude ranchers and some trail riders.

Do you ride English or Western?

TYPES OF TACK

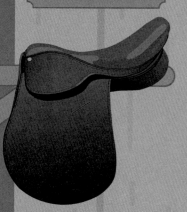

BRIDLE
The bridle is the rider's main source of communication and control with the horse.

RACING SADDLE

ENDURANCE SADDLE

BIT
A bit attaches to the bridle and goes in the horse's mouth to assist with the rider's communication with the horse.

JUMPING SADDLE

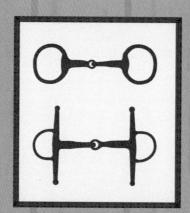

DRESSAGE SADDLE

SADDLE SEAT SADDLE

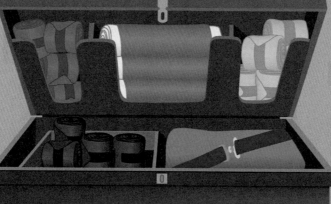

TACK TRUNK

PARTS OF THE BRIDLE

Throatlatch

Headpiece

Browband

Cheek Piece

Noseband

Bit

Reins

PARTS OF THE SADDLE

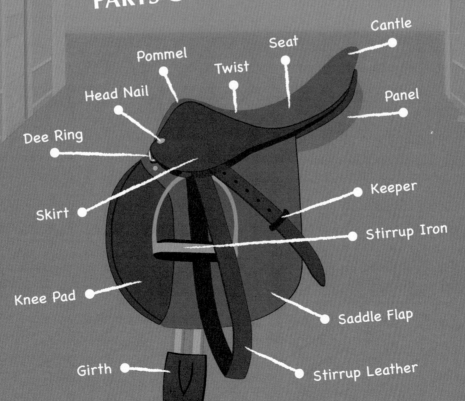

Cantle

Seat

Pommel

Twist

Head Nail

Panel

Dee Ring

Keeper

Skirt

Stirrup Iron

Knee Pad

Saddle Flap

Girth

Stirrup Leather

TACK CROSSWORD PUZZLE

You always walk a horse on the left side, and mount and dismount from the left side.

WORD BANK

BIT	SKIRT	BROWBAND	POMMEL	STIRRUP IRON
NOSE BAND	CANTLE	KEEPER	CHEEK PIECE	KNEEPAD
TWIST	THROATLATCH	PANEL	REINS	

ACROSS

DOWN

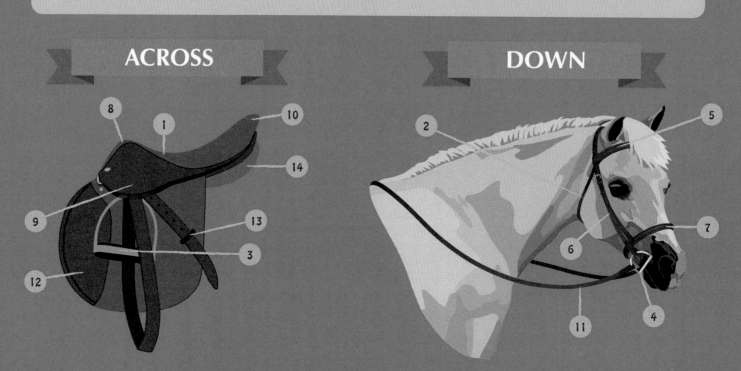

PARTS OF THE HORSE

A horse's conformation is the way a horse is built. Good conformation improves movement and performance, allows for smoother gaits and makes horses and ponies less likely to go lame.

GOOD CONFORMATION

- Large kind eyes
- Wide Jaw
- Large nostrils
- Medium-length neck that is slightly arched
- Long, sloping shoulder
- Well-muscled back
- Pasterns are a medium length & slope

CONFORMATION FAULTS

- Large, course head
- Small "pig eyes"
- Narrow jaw
- Small nostrils
- Neck that dips on the top & bulges on the bottom (ewe neck)
- Short, upright shoulders
- Long, sway back

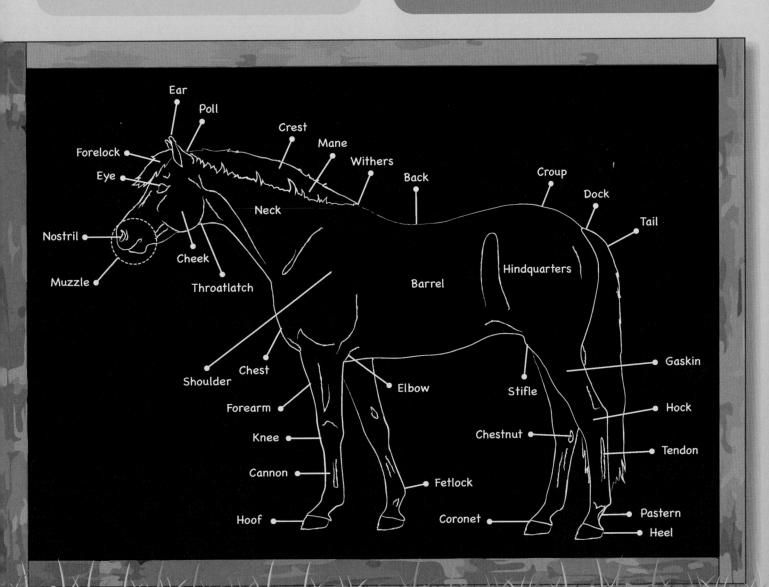

PARTS OF THE HORSE ACTIVITY

Finish writing the names of the parts of the horse.

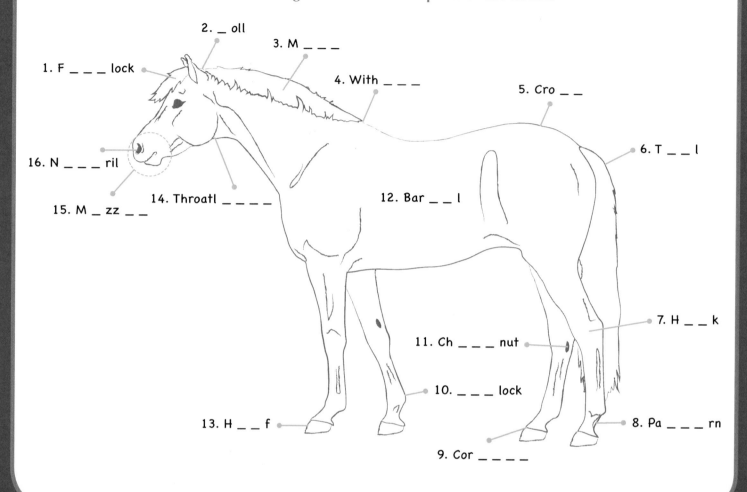

2. _ oll

3. M _ _ _

1. F _ _ _ lock

4. With _ _ _

5. Cro _ _

6. T _ _ l

16. N _ _ _ ril

15. M _ zz _ _

14. Throatl _ _ _ _

12. Bar _ _ l

11. Ch _ _ _ nut

10. _ _ _ lock

13. H _ _ f

7. H _ _ k

8. Pa _ _ _ rn

9. Cor _ _ _ _

PARTS OF THE HORSE WORD SEARCH

Find and circle the words in the list. Words can be found across or down.

S	T	A	I	L	F	C	A	E	M	C
F	M	A	N	E	E	A	N	K	A	R
E	U	L	W	I	T	H	E	R	S	E
T	Z	I	I	T	L	W	T	I	C	S
O	Z	K	T	C	O	R	O	N	E	T
O	L	H	Y	U	C	U	N	E	S	L
F	E	O	C	Z	K	M	E	T	R	A
H	O	C	K	W	H	O	O	F	E	Z

WORD BANK

WITHERS

FETLOCK

HOCK

CREST

MUZZLE

TAIL

CORONET

HOOF

MANE

HORSE BARN MAZE

Help the horse find his barn. Do not go past anything blocking his path.

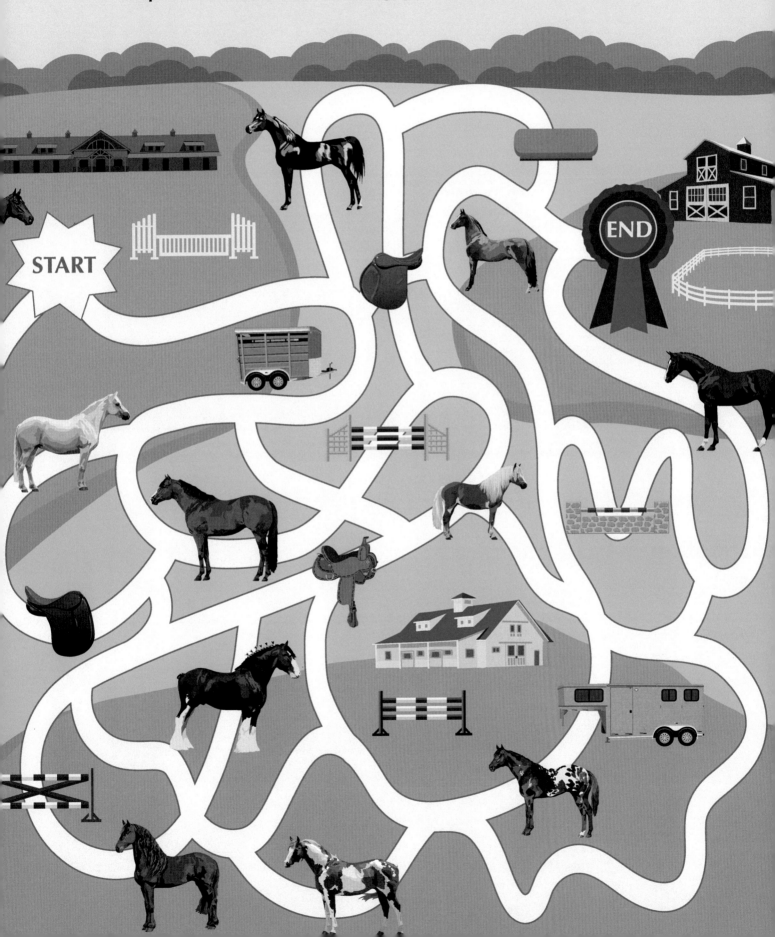

HIDDEN PICTURES

Can you find these objects in the big picture?

HORSE & PONY TERMS

Foal: A baby horse or pony under 1 year old.

Yearling: A horse or pony who is 1 year old.

Colt: A young MALE horse/pony under 4 years old.

Filly: A young FEMALE horse/pony under 4 years old.

Dam: The MOTHER of a horse/pony.

Sire: The FATHER of a horse/pony.

Stallion: A MALE horse/pony who is 4 years old or older. He can be used for breeding.

Gelding: A MALE horse/pony, of any age, who has been neutered. He cannot be used for breeding.

Mare: A FEMALE horse/pony who is 4 years old or older.

MEASURE A HORSE'S HEIGHT

Horses and ponies are measured in **"hands"**. A hand is **4 inches** and is the approximate width of the palm of an adult's hand. Horses and ponies are measured from the ground straight up to the withers.

HORSE & PONY HEIGHTS:

- The shortest a horse can be is 14.3 hands high (hh); otherwise the animal will be categorized as a pony.

- The tallest a pony can be is 14.2 hh

- A SMALL pony measures up to 12.2 hh

- A MEDIUM pony measures from 12.2 hh to 13.2 hh

- A LARGE pony measures from 13.2 hh to 14.2 hh

How wide is the palm of your hand?

1   2   3   4

TYING A PONY

Always tie a horse with a quick release knot so the horse can be untied quickly in an emergency.

Keep in mind when tying a horse:

- Use a breakaway halter and tie the pony at the height of his withers or higher. The pony should be able to hold his head in a relaxed position. If the lead rope is too loose, he could get his legs tangled. 18" is a good length from the halter to the knot.

- For safety, tie a piece of baling twine to the ring or post, and loop the lead rope through it. The twine is strong enough to hold the pony under normal conditions, but will break if the pony spooks and pulls back really hard.

- Never tie a pony with a chain over his nose or under his chin, or tie him by his bridle. He could injure himself if he pulls back.

- To undo a quick release knot, pull the loose end and the knot will untie on its own.

How to tie a quick release knot:

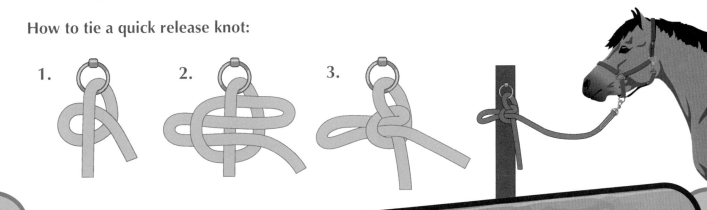

1.   2.   3.

PRACTICE TYING A QUICK RELEASE KNOT

1. Have an adult attach a rope or string to something sturdy, such as the leg of a chair.

2. Practice tying a quick release knot following the steps above.

3. Release the knot by pulling on the loose end.

4. Repeat until you can easily tie and release a quick release knot.

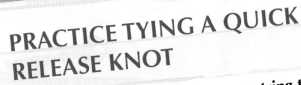

HORSE & PONY COAT COLORS

Some common coat colors include:

CHESTNUT

BUCKSKIN

LIVER CHESTNUT

BAY

FLAXEN CHESTNUT

DARK BAY

PALOMINO

BLACK

A pony's coat color means the color of his body and head, as well as his mane and tail. Coat colors are used to identify horses and describe how they look, along with face and leg markings.

GRAY

STRAWBERRY ROAN

FLEA-BITTEN GRAY

BLUE ROAN

DAPPLE GRAY

PINTO

GRULLA

APPALOOSA

A HORSE OF A DIFFERENT COLOR

Find you favorite horse & pony coat color in the border,
then draw your own picture of it below.

A flea-bitten grey
horse has a light
grey coat with
speckles of
chestnut hairs

In the border, put a check next to each of the
different horse & pony coat colors you have seen.

FACE MARKINGS

Face Markings are the white markings on the horse or pony's face and muzzle. They are important for identification and registration by breed societies.

Bald Face: A wide white marking that runs past the inside of the eyes and beyond the nostrils.

Blaze: A white marking that occurs below the eye line and above the top of the nostrils, and extends outside of both nasal bones.

Star: A white marking that occurs above the eye line.

Strip: A white marking that occurs below the eye line and above the top of the nostrils, but within the nasal bones.

Snip: A white marking that occurs between the top and the bottom of the nostrils.

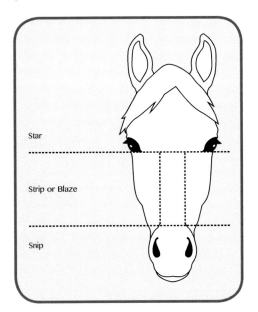

Star

Strip or Blaze

Snip

BALD FACE

BLAZE

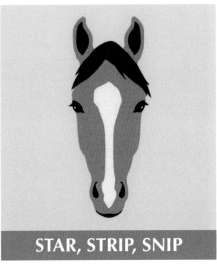

STAR, STRIP, SNIP

STAR, STRIP

STAR

SNIP

NAME THE FACE MARKINGS

Color in the horse heads and write in the name of the correct face markings on each line.

LEG MARKINGS

Leg markings are described by how far up the white extends on a horse's or pony's leg.

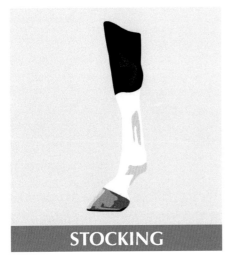

STOCKING

Stocking: A white leg marking that extends all the way up the cannon bone.

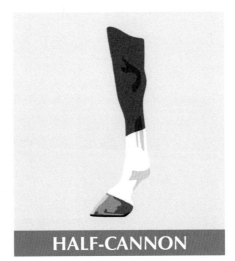

HALF-CANNON

Half-Cannon: A white leg marking that extends up half of the cannon bone.

SOCK

Sock: A white leg marking that covers all of the pastern and over the fetlock joint.

HALF-PASTERN

Half-Pastern: A white leg marking that covers half of the pastern.

CORONET

Coronet: Thin white marking that runs near the top of the hoof along the coronet band.

ERMINE SPOTS

Ermine Spots: Small dark spots that appear on any white marking near the hoof.

OTHER MARKS

Brand: A design burned into the horse that is usually used to identify the animal with a breed.

Freeze Brand: A brand made by freezing instead of burning, usually on the neck. Numbers and letters are usually used, and the hair grows back in white.

GAITS

Gaits are the ways in which a horse or pony can move, either naturally or through training.

WALK

The walk is a gait with four beats. It does not have a moment of suspension and averages 4 mph.

1st Beat: Right Hind Leg
2nd Beat: Right Fore Leg
3rd Beat: Left Hind Leg
4th Beat: Left Fore Leg

TROT

The trot has two beats, averages 6 mph and has a moment of suspension. The horse's legs move in diagonal pairs.

1st Beat: Left Fore Leg/ Right Hind Leg
2nd Beat: Right Fore Leg/ Left Hind Leg

CANTER

The canter has three beats, averages 8 mph, and has a moment of suspension.

LEFT LEAD The left front leg leads when cantering on the left lead.

1st Beat: Right Hind Leg
2nd Beat: Left Hind Leg/ Right Fore Leg
3rd Beat: Left Fore Leg

RIGHT LEAD The right front leg leads when cantering on the right lead.

1st Beat: Left Hind Leg
2nd Beat: Right Hind Leg/ Left Fore Leg
3rd Beat: Right Fore Leg

CONNECT THE DOTS

Connect the dots to make a horse. Can you identify the horse's gait? What lead is he on?

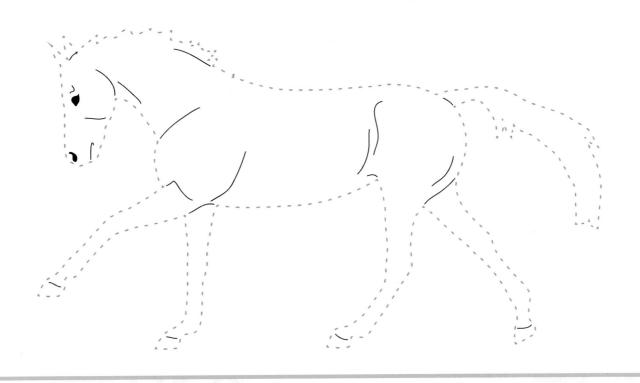

TROT FLIP BOOK

Cut out each rectangle and arrange the pages in order with 1 on top. Staple the left edge. Hold the book on the left edge and brush your thumb over the right edges to make the book flip.

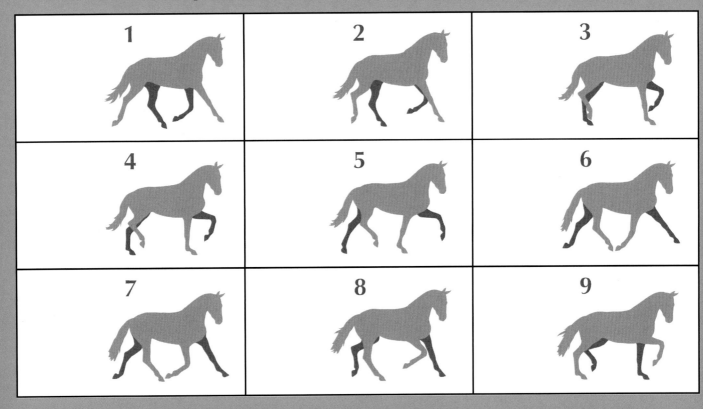

RIDING SPORTS

Some popular riding sports include:

HUNTER JUMPER

Hunter Jumper shows are divided into hunters, equitation, and jumpers. Hunters are judged on manners, way of going, and conformation. Jumpers have more speed than hunters and are judged on jumping ability over a timed course. Equitation classes judge the rider's position and overall effectiveness.

WESTERN PLEASURE

Western Pleasure is a Western style competition where the horses appear to be a pleasure to ride, look very smooth and collected, and have minimal rein contact.

POLO

Polo is a team sport played on a grass field that consists of four riders. The objective is to score goals by hitting a small ball into the opposing team's goal using a long-handled mallet

EVENTING

Eventing is an Olympic sport where horse and rider teams compete over three days in dressage, show jumping, and cross-country.

SADDLE SEAT

Saddle Seat riding is an English sport with energetic and high-stepping horses that are smooth and comfortable to ride. The rider sits toward the back of the saddle and carries the hands high.

DRESSAGE

Dressage means training in French. It is an Olympic sport where a horse responds to subtle aides from the rider to perform a series of movements in a standard arena.

EVENTING MATCH GAME

Eventing is an Olympic sport where horse and rider teams compete over three days in dressage, show jumping, and cross-country.

Circle the matching silhouette under each eventing phase.

DRESSAGE   **CROSS-COUNTRY**   **SHOW JUMPING**

HORSE BREEDS

Horse breeds are groups of horses with similar characteristics that are passed down to their offspring. Some popular horse breeds include:

APPALOOSA

WARMBLOOD

LIPIZZAN

FRIESIAN

QUARTER HORSE

THOROUGHBRED

MORGAN

PAINT OR PINTO

CLYDESDALE

ARABIAN

HOT BLOOD, COLD BLOOD & WARMBLOOD HORSES

There are more than 150 breeds of horses and ponies worldwide. Horse & pony breeds have been developed to fulfill various needs, such as: pulling heavy loads, racing or teaching children how to ride.

All horses are warm-blooded mammals. They can also can be classified by their temperaments and body types. Arabian and Thoroughbred horses fall into the "hot blood" category because they are usually more sensitive, high strung, and have lighter body types than other breeds of horses. "Cold blood" horses include the draft breeds, such as: Shires, Clydesdales, Percherons and even Friesians. These large and sturdy breeds have been bred for agricultural work and are chosen for their calm temperaments.

"Warmblood" horses are a cross between the hot blood and cold blood breeds. They usually have calmer temperaments than Thoroughbreds and Arabians and have more athletic ability than their cold-blooded ancestors. They are used today for dressage, jumping, eventing and driving.

The difference between ponies and horses is their height. Ponies are no taller than 14.2 hands high (58 inches) at the withers, while horses are taller than 14.2 hands high.

PONY BREEDS

Some popular pony breeds include:

SHETLAND PONY

WELSH PONY

CONNEMARA

HAFLINGER

COLOR BY NUMBER

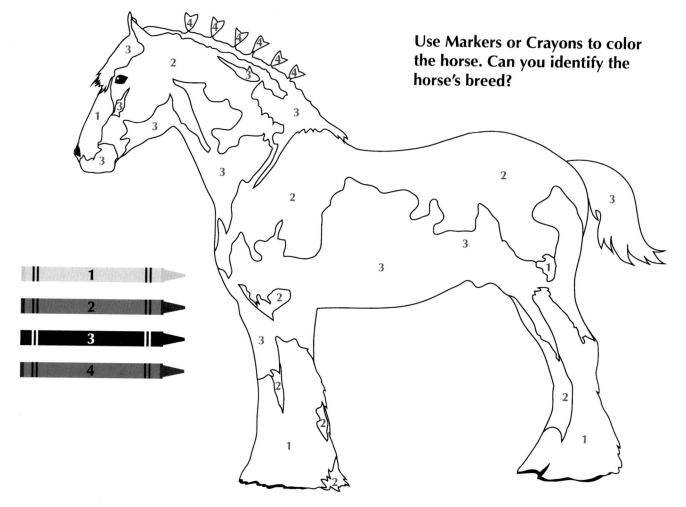

Use Markers or Crayons to color the horse. Can you identify the horse's breed?

HORSE BREEDS QUIZ

1. Which type of horse is a cross between hot and cold-blood breeds?

- ☐ Clydesdale
- ☐ Mammal
- ☐ Hanovarian
- ☐ Warmblood

2. Name a cold-blood horse breed.

- ☐ Friesian
- ☐ Arabian
- ☐ Morgan
- ☐ Shetland

3. Name two hot-blood horse breeds.

- ☐ Arabian
- ☐ Clydesdale
- ☐ Thoroughbred
- ☐ Connemara

4. Which breed has long, lean bodies, are sensitive, and can be high strung?

- ☐ Warmblood
- ☐ Welsh Pony
- ☐ Quarter Horse
- ☐ Thoroughbred

DESCRIBE YOUR PONY

It is important to be able to correctly describe your horse or pony using correct terms, in case someone unfamiliar with your animal needs to retrieve him from a group of other horses, or if your horse or pony gets loose and you need to describe him. When describing a horse or pony, include characteristics such as: height, age, color, breed, gender – and any markings or distinguishing marks, such as brands or scars.

Examples of horse and pony characteristics:

HEIGHT	AGE	COLOR	BREED	GENDER	MARKINGS
15.2 hh	14 year-old	Chestnut	Quarter Horse	Mare	Stocking on LF
12.1 hh	6 year-old	Dapple Grey	Welsh Pony	Gelding	Star
14.2 hh	2 year-old	Bay	Arabian	Colt	Blaze

Example description: "Daisy is a 15 year-old dark bay Hanovarian mare, who is 16 hands tall with a star, strip & snip. She has a sock on her left hind and a stocking on her right hind, with a scar above her right front fetlock."

Write a complete description of a horse or pony:

_____

_____

Color in the blank pony below to resemble the one you described:

ANSWERS

PICTURE SEARCH

Left to right: Pages 17, 22, 13, 24, 4.

HORSE BARN MAZE

GROOMING TOOLS MATCH GAME

Top to bottom: Hoof pick, mane comb, body brush, dandy brush, curry comb.

TACK CROSSWORD PUZZLE

1. Twist, 2. Throatlatch, 3. Stirrup Iron, 4. Bit, 5. Browband, 6. Cheek Piece, 7. Nose Band, 8. Pommel, 9. Skirt, 10. Cantle, 11. Reins, 12. Kneepad, 13. Keeper, 14. Panel

HORSE BARN MAZE

PARTS OF THE HORSE ACTIVITY

1. Fetlock, 2. Poll, 3. Mane, 4. Withers, 5. Croup, 6. Tail, 7. Hock, 8. Pastern, 9. Coronet, 10. Fetlock, 11. Chestnut, 12. Barrel, 14. Throatlatch, 15. Muzzle, 16. Nostril

PARTS OF THE HORSE WORD SEARCH

HIDDEN PICTURES

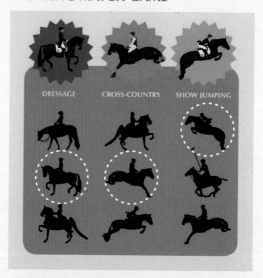

NAME THE FACE MARKINGS

Left to right, top to bottom: Bald face, Blaze, Star Strip Snip, Star Strip, Star, Star Snip, Snip.

CONNECT THE DOTS

Canter, Left lead.

EVENTING MATCH GAME

COLOR BY NUMBER

Clydesdale

HORSE BREEDS QUIZ

1. Warmbloods 2. Friesian 3. Arabian, Thoroughbred 4. Thoroughbred

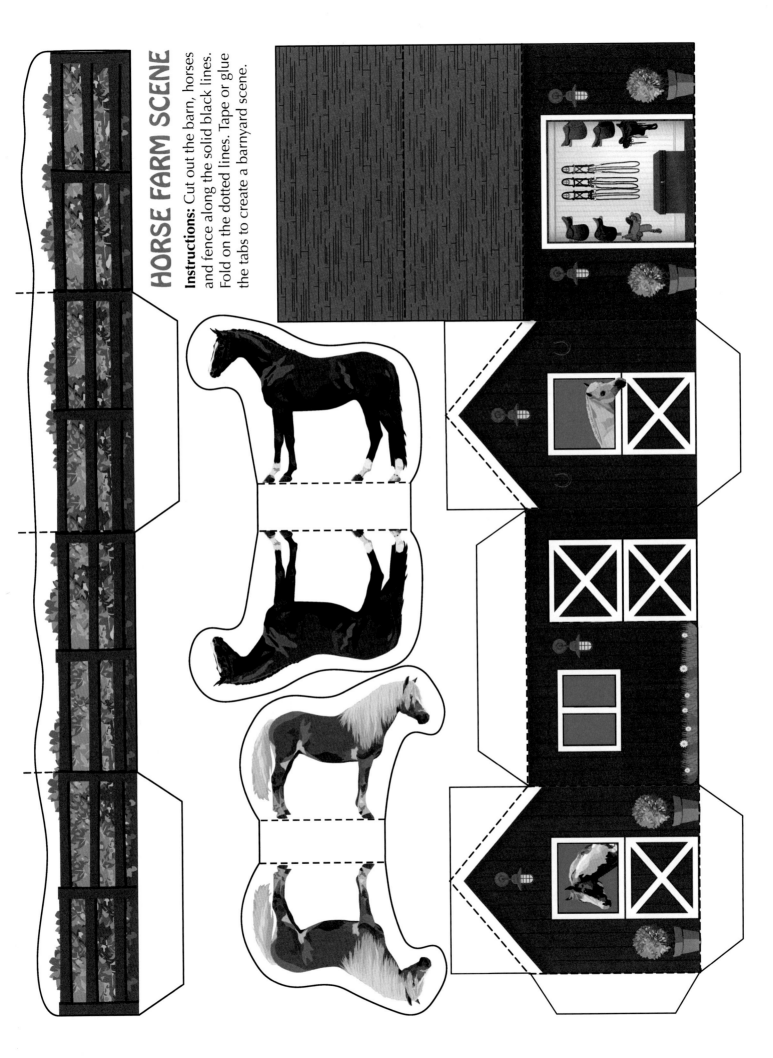

HORSE FARM SCENE

Instructions: Cut out the barn, horses and fence along the solid black lines. Fold on the dotted lines. Tape or glue the tabs to create a barnyard scene.

ABOUT THE AUTHOR

Susan DiFelice is a digital designer & fine artist with 20 years of experience working with large corporations, universities, and small businesses in addition to painting animal portraits. Susan and her husband live in Chapel Hill, NC with their two children where she works in between taxiing children and time at the barn. As a life-long rider, Susan developed Allpony and this activity book to marry her web, graphic design and fine art skills with her love of riding to teach her own children about horsemanship. It has grown from there and has become a resource for other horse-crazy kids.

First Printing: 2017

ISBN 978-1973830863

PO Box 189
Chapel Hill, NC 27514

www.allpony.com

Made in the USA
Lexington, KY
09 April 2018